A WALK IN JERUSALEM

A
WALK *in*
JERUSALEM
STATIONS *of the* CROSS

JOHN L. PETERSON

MOREHOUSE PUBLISHING

Morehouse Publishing, 4775 Linglestown Road, Harrisburg, PA 17112
Morehouse Publishing, 445 Fifth Avenue, New York, NY 10016
Morehouse Publishing is an imprint of Church Publishing Incorporated.

A Walk in Jerusalem: Stations of the Cross was produced at St. Gregory's College in
Jerusalem.

The late **Brother Gilbert Sinden**, a Course Director at the College, wrote liturgies for the
first through the thirteenth Stations of the Cross; however, he did not write the liturgy
for the fourteenth station, but always used the "Confessions" and "Healings" that are
included in this book every time he did the Stations of the Cross in Jerusalem. Every
effort to discover the author of that material has proved fruitless so far, and the publisher
would be grateful for any information about its provenance so that proper credit may be given.

Barbara Huston, former course member at St. George's College and riter for the
College, was the original editor of the text; **Margaret Dewey**, former librarian of the
College, provided key research on the Stations of the Cross.

Illustrations and map are courtesy of architect **Donald Neraas**, member of the College's
North American Regional Committee.

Photographs are courtesy of **Garo Nalbandian**.

Cover design by Corey Kent.

Printed in the United States of America.

Library of Congress Cataloging-in-Publication Data
Peterson, John L.
    A walk in Jerusalem : stations of the Cross / John L. Peterson
        p. cm.
    ISBN 13 : 978-0-8192-1735-6
    1. Stations of the Cross. 2. Christian pilgrims and pilgrimage—Jerusalem.
3. Jerusalem—Description and travel. I. Title
BX2040.P45   1998
232.96—dc21   97-44727
                                                                CIP

CONTENTS

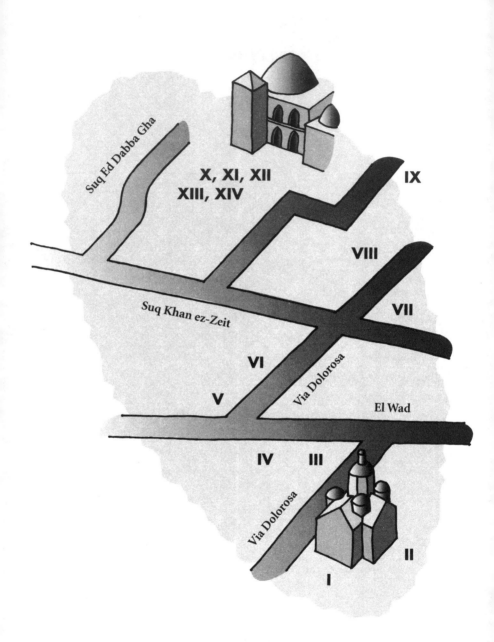

Suq Ed Dabba Gha

X, XI, XII
XIII, XIV

IX

VIII

VII

Suq Khan ez-Zeit

VI

V

Via Dolorosa

El Wad

IV   III

Via Dolorosa

II

I

Stations of the Cross

INTRODUCTION

NO ROAD IN THE HOLY LAND HAS BEEN MORE TRAVELED than the Way of the Cross in Jerusalem. It is an ecumenical phenomenon and never more so than today.

Franciscan monks in their brown robes lead groups along the route every Friday. Cruise-ship holiday groups in identical hats may be seen there any day of the week in tourist season. Pilgrims singing hymns in many languages are heard there. The Stations of the Cross is everyone's sacrament in the city where Christ actually was forced to his own crucifixion.

This book walks us through the Way of the Cross in Jerusalem with rites born in Jerusalem. We mark where Jesus Is Judged, Jesus Receives His Cross, Jesus Falls for the First Time, Jesus Meets His Mother, Simon of Cyrene Helps Jesus Carry the Cross, Veronica Wipes Jesus' Brow, Jesus Falls a Second Time, Jesus Talks to the Weeping Women, Jesus Falls a Third Time, Jesus Is Stripped of His Garments, Jesus Is Crucified, Jesus Dies on the Cross, Jesus' Body Is Taken Down from the Cross, and Jesus' Body Is Placed in the Tomb.

We have made this walk for centuries one way and another, feeling it with our feet and living it in our hearts. We have thus transformed it into a folk sacrament, complete with its outward and visible sign of an inward and spiritual grace.

A twentieth-century Way of the Cross is mapped on the opposite page.

What is its history? The first record of this pilgrim practice, walking the Way of the Cross in Jerusalem after the death and resurrection of Christ, comes from the Spanish pilgrim Egeria. In 381 and 384 A.D. she made a Good Friday pilgrimage from the Mount of Olives to the

Church of the Holy Sepulchre. This church, built over the site of Christ's crucifixion and burial, was already the Christian focal point in Jerusalem during Holy Week that it is today. On Good Friday, during Egeria's two visits, everyone spent three hours in the church hearing the Psalms and readings from the Epistles, the Acts, the Gospels, and other prophetic words connected with the Passion.

Such outdoor processions as Egeria's did not thrive in subsequent non-Christian rule in Jerusalem. Still, six liturgical stations on a processional route from the Mount of Olives to the Church of the Holy Sepulchre were described in tenth-century Holy Week records. The processional cross would then be carried within the church, from the Calvary site on the mezzanine floor to a small cave in the ancient stone quarry pit below, a cave known as the "holy prison."

When the European Crusaders reached Jerusalem in the eleventh century, they found the Passion honored only as a Good Friday ceremony in a partially rebuilt Church of the Holy Sepulchre whose original had been destroyed in 1009. What had once been outdoor Stations of the Cross were now interior chapels honoring Christ's scourging, his crowning with thorns, and the dividing of his garments.

The Crusaders enthusiastically rebuilt the Church of the Holy Sepulchre and added others between it and the Mount of Olives, including one in Gethsemane, where the Church of All Nations now stands. The Crusaders focused on the Church of the Holy Sepulchre, however, because they preferred the story of Christ's death and resurrection to his Passion. No public procession was ever scheduled for Good Friday during the Crusader period.

After the European Christians departed from the Holy Land in 1291, the Franciscan Order of Monks remained to care for its Christian places. The end of the Crusades failed to discourage pilgrims from landing on the Holy Land's Mediterranean shore where Franciscan monks could lead them, by donkey, thirty-nine miles inland to Jerusalem. In those days processions for the Way of the Cross varied greatly. One Italian pilgrim said he went from the Mount of Olives through the present St. Stephen's Gate, sometimes called Lion's Gate, past Islam's golden Dome of the Rock to St. Anne's Church, the Via Dolorosa, and the Church of the Holy Sepulchre. Later medieval pilgrims reported processing in the opposite direction, from the Holy Sepulchre at daybreak to Gethsemane, the Mount of Olives, and Mount Zion.

Pilgrims could be locked into the Church of the Holy Sepulchre overnight and process among its many chapels, eating and sleeping there. The duration of their visit depended on their piety and on the patience of the Muslim family that always held the church keys. In the fifteenth century, English pilgrim Margery Kemp had herself locked in the Church for twenty-four hours, but most pilgrims just stayed overnight. They might, however, return for more than one night.

Meanwhile, the Crusaders had taken the idea of Stations of the Cross home to Europe, where murderous struggles between Church and State, wars among nations, the Black Death, and famine had given the people of medieval times a new appreciation for Christ's suffering, death, and resurrection. These particular attributes of Christ became the principal focus of medieval spirituality. Walking his Way of the Cross was a meaningful expression of the penitent's pain and of ultimate healing through resurrection.

Other forms the drama took in Europe were passion plays such as the one performed at Oberammergau, Germany. First presented in 1634 in thanksgiving for deliverance from the Black Death, it continues to the present day. Artists such as El Greco, Jan van Eyck, Fra Angelico, Michelangelo, and Rembrandt expressed the Passion in paint, bas-relief, and sculpture. Religious men and women wrote about it. Julian of Norwich described her vision of Christ's wounds. In *The Imitation of Christ*, Thomas a Kempis invited readers to take refuge in the wounds of the Savior, to undertake the holy Way of the Cross.

Through the centuries, this mystical path was also called the sorrowful way, *via crucis*, the "mournful way," or the "very painful way." Stations of the Cross, built like stage sets along a path, sprang up in medieval European towns and were given such names as the Seven Falls, the Seven Pillars, the Sorrowful Journey, the Way of Affliction, or the Holy Way par excellence.

"Those who cannot go there in person can still make this voyage by the grace of God, through devout and pious meditations as follow," wrote Jan Pascha in his 1563 book, *Spiritual Journey*, describing the Stations of the Cross in Louvain, Belgium. "You will find here the holy places as clearly depicted as if before your very eyes, all shown by the descriptions of pilgrims, who have themselves been personally to these same holy places," Pascha wrote.

Perhaps the most famous set of stations in Europe, the Louvain group has been called the original of today's Way of the Cross because the stations, eight bas-relief pictures, begin with a "Pilate's House" and end in Calvary. Other famous stations in France, Switzerland, Italy, Spain, Belgium, Holland, Germany, Austria, and Hungary had different station names and numbers.

You can imagine the confusion, therefore, when European pilgrims visited Jerusalem and sought to reconcile their European "passion play" with Jerusalem itself. In 1725, Franciscan Eleazar Horn drew a map of Jerusalem showing fourteen stations (some located differently than today) to which Jerusalem's Franciscans began to lead the Friday afternoon pilgrimage we still see today. Nine of the stations come from the Gospels. Five come from medieval European imagination: Jesus' three falls, his meeting his mother, and Veronica wiping his face.

The Stations of the Cross in Jerusalem today lead right through the busy marketplace; pilgrims are as uncloistered and unprotected as Jesus was on the first Good Friday. Our senses are assaulted with the sound of children shouting, Muslim muezzin chanting from their minarets, merchants calling tourists, tourists talking, and car horns honking. We smell lamb broiling, falafel cooking, and heaters burning. We see exotic fruit stands, small carts delivering construction materials or pastries, mysterious faces, rivulets of water slowly running down the concave center of the street, and unknown side streets leading into shadows.

All sorts and conditions of people are walking this Way at any hour of the day on any day of the year. Among them are those who come to St. George's College located just outside the walled Old City of Jerusalem. Founded for British and Palestinian priesthood candidates, the College has become an international, ecumenical, continuing education center for everyone who wishes to spend ten days to ten weeks becoming acquainted with the Bible's landmarks under the leadership of experts in its archaeology, texts, geography, history, and spirituality.

Director of these courses at St. George's College from 1979 to 1989 was the late Bro. Gilbert Sinden, SSM, who wrote the liturgy of prayers in this book. A priest of the Anglican Society of the Sacred Mission, Sinden had already edited a new Australian Prayer Book. Though

English-born, in 1929, Gilbert became an Australian citizen and died on duty there in 1990.

Bro. Gilbert was a beloved figure of wide girth, with the gift of revealing the Bible and the Church so that "you suddenly understood what you had not known before," as a friend said. "I remember once he took me to the top of the Mount of Olives and we said Morning Prayer, while behind us the sun came up and illuminated Jerusalem before us, as Gilbert could illuminate Jerusalem in one's mind."

Though he had taught Old and New Testament courses for twenty years elsewhere, "experience of the geographical reality of the Land of the Bible can give one a radically different perspective on the Bible," Gilbert once wrote. "I went looking for a top dressing on what I already knew; I leave ashamed that I had presumed to teach for so long out of so much ignorance."

And who knows, friends say now, how many people he helped through difficulties, how many were strengthened in their faith, how many learned a new respect for themselves, because of his immense and costly care for them. He had always battled tenaciously for the underdog, for the rejected, and for the devalued. In Palestine/Israel he had a passionate concern for justice and peace for all people who share that land.

"This is not the place to rehearse the details of the tragic situation in the Holy Land, but no attempt to reflect on my years there can ignore the devastation in my mind and heart which that conflict between two contradictory kinds of justice has wrought," he wrote. "For I found myself living with a people to whom the simplest natural justice has been, and still is being, denied in order to do justice to another people to whom they have done so much less harm than the rest of us.

"I thank God for Jewish friends who boldly tell their fellow Jews that the Palestinians deserve the same identity, security, dignity, and homeland that they themselves deserve; and for Palestinian friends who recognize the horrors of the Holocaust and steadfastly seek a balance of the two kinds of justice the two peoples each need, knowing perfectly well that this will mean real sacrifices on their part."

The longer Gilbert stayed in Jerusalem, during those ten years at St. George's College, the more difficult he found it to pray. "This is difficult to describe because it was so unexpected, but I have come to think that it has much to do with the history of Jerusalem, and not least with the

fact that it was here that Jesus was crucified: the cosmic conflict that
raged around the cross seems to have raged in this city throughout all
generations, and no less so today. Those who try to pray here find themselves caught up in that conflict: 'I thirst;' 'My God, why have you aban-
doned me?,' 'Father, forgive…'"

I dedicate this book to Gilbert in part because he wrote its liturgies,
which we used every time we did the Stations of the Cross during my
whole tenure as Dean of St. George's College from 1983 through 1994.
I also dedicate it to him because it was Gilbert who instilled in me a
deep love for the Stations of the Cross and a passion for the Church of
the Holy Sepulchre.

I also dedicate this book to all those men and women who have stud-
ied at St. George's College in the past, are studying there now, and will
do so in the future. When I was Dean of the College, I led so many of
them over the familiar stones of the Via Dolorosa. I told them about the
stations. We said the prayers. We sang hymns. We took turns carrying a
wooden cross.

And I dedicate this book, as well, to all readers who cannot go to
Jerusalem in body but who, in heart and mind, can walk the Stations of
the Cross.

But most important, I dedicate this book to Kirsten, who shares my
love of Jerusalem and who walked the stations with Gilbert, and to
Emily and Carrie, who indeed will always be children of Jerusalem.

The liturgy can, of course, be said at Stations of the Cross anywhere
in the world, in the quiet of your own room, as a Lenten devotion in a
parish church, or at a place of devotion and prayer. We are all citizens
of Jerusalem.

John L. Peterson
Secretary General
The Anglican Communion
London 1998

STATION I
Jesus Is Judged

So Pilate, wishing to satisfy the crowd, released Barabbas for them; and after flogging Jesus, he handed him over to be crucified.

Then the soldiers led him into the courtyard of the palace (that is, the governor's headquarters, called Praetorium in Greek), and they called together the whole cohort. And they clothed him in a purple cloak; and after twisting some thorns into a crown, they put it on him.

—Mark 15:15–17

JESUS HAD BEEN ARRESTED THE PREVIOUS EVENING in the Garden of Gethsemane on the Mount of Olives, at the instigation of the Jewish leaders in Jerusalem. Those who caused his arrest were unable to convict Jesus of any capital crime by their own laws. They were forced to bring him before the Roman governor on a charge of rebellion against the occupying power, Rome.

Roman Governor Pontius Pilate is uncomfortable with the whole situation. The crowd is unruly. The quiet dignity and calm assurance of the prisoner disturbs Pilate profoundly, but he is too weak to stand up to the crowd. Their shouts of "Crucify him!" become louder and louder. Finally the governor yields, and he sentences Jesus to death by crucifixion, the terrible death reserved for slaves, pirates, and rebels against the state.

The governor orders him to be scourged first. Scourging consists of a beating with a many-thonged whip, each thong tipped with a metal

STATION I. JESUS IS JUDGED

pellet. The beating is administered as a grim kind of mercy to weaken the condemned man so as to shorten his suffering on the cross.

Many scholars believe that this judgment of Jesus would have taken place where Pontius Pilate was staying that fateful day when he came down from his home in Caesarea to keep watch over the Passover crowds. Had Pilate been staying at the Jewish King Herod's palace, the judgment would have taken place there, where the Jaffa Gate is now located. Then Jesus' Via Dolorosa would actually have led down the Decamanius (now David Street) to the Cardo (now Suq Khan ez-Zeit) and out the city gate of that day to Golgotha, sometimes called Calvary, where the Church of the Holy Sepulchre is now.

If Pilate stayed with the Roman troops at the Antonia Fortress, as the Crusaders decided he had done, then Jesus was judged there and walked the path that we follow today, the Via Dolorosa route mapped in this book. The ancient Antonia Fortress, now the Omariye Muslim College, normally is not available for use, however, because school is in session. Thus the Franciscan monks in Jerusalem open their Church of the Flagellation for the pilgrims.

I particularly like this church because of the crown-of-thorns mosaic on the sanctuary dome, which really sets our theme. Kings and queens in today's world do not wear crowns of thorns. They wear crowns of gold, silver, and other precious metals, set with diamonds, emeralds, rubies, and other precious stones. But the King of Kings and Lord of Lords, our King, wears a crown of thorns, a crown that pierces the skin, a crown that causes blood to flow. As we come to this First Station of the Cross we are confronted head-on with a divine reversal. God turns everything we hold so precious absolutely upside down. All the things that we hold so dear—wealth, power, security—are replaced by a crown of thorns. Everything that seems to give us meaning in life—authority, prestige, our own self-importance—is turned upside down by a crown of thorns. It is here at the First Station of the Cross that we see the divine reversal as God's Son wears a crown of thorns.

We will ask ourselves during these fourteen Stations of the Cross whether we are willing to be a disciple of Jesus. How willing are we to wear a crown of thorns?

Let us pray:

For politicians, statespersons, government officials, leaders,
especially those in our own countries, that they may seek
the common good—peace, equity, and justice;
For judges and magistrates, that they may administer true justice
impartially and with mercy;
For those who have power of life and death over others;
For every occasion when human beings use their skill to hurt and kill;

Lord have mercy.
Christ have mercy.
Lord have mercy.

Let us pray:

For those condemned to death for whatever reason;
For those imprisoned, lawfully and unlawfully, justly and unjustly;
For those serving very long or indeterminate sentences;

Lord have mercy.
Christ have mercy.
Lord have mercy.

Let us pray:

For ourselves;
When we judge others, and for those we condemn;
When we stand judged or condemned, rightly or wrongly;
That we may know the witness and humility of Christ;

Lord have mercy.
Christ have mercy.
Lord have mercy.

STATION II
Jesus Receives His Cross

So they took Jesus; and carrying the cross by himself, he went out to what is called The Place of the Skull, which in Aramaic is called Golgotha.

—John 19:16b–17

WHILE THEY ARE WAITING FOR THOSE WHOM THEY WILL CRUCIFY to be brought from their cells, the soldiers in the execution detail idle the time away with a rough gambling game. They see Jesus as a condemned terrorist whose activities threaten their very lives. So they unhesitantly gamble for the privilege of tormenting him along the way with blows and words.

When the condemned men appear—there are three of them—each receives a single beam to carry across his shoulders to Golgotha. A placard declaring each man's crime will be carried in front of him. The death procession forms, and the order is given to move out through the crowded streets.

At this second station, the Church of the Condemnation, adjacent to the Church of the Flagellation, we actually stand on the beveled flagstones of a Roman road in Jerusalem. While most of the time we will not be walking where Jesus placed his own feet that day, this is one of the few places in Jerusalem where there is original Roman pavement. In most other places we will be walking approximately sixteen feet above the original path.

As we walk the stations today, let us think about those sixteen feet. Every single millimeter, every single inch of dirt on which we walk includes the dust from the shoes and the tears from the eyes of pilgrims. They—we—

STATION II. JESUS RECEIVES HIS CROSS

weep for the prisoner condemned as The King of the Jews, "despised and rejected," carrying so much more than a heavy, bruising, rough beam of wood. He is "enduring the suffering that should have been ours, the pain that we should have borne."

Are we going to leave granules of dirt on our path through our own Jerusalem? We leave grains when we walk across the street to help someone in need, to hold the hand of someone who needs us—when we do anything Christlike.

Let us pray:

For all police officers, prison officers, and those required to carry out death sentences and corporal punishment;

Lord have mercy.
Christ have mercy.
Lord have mercy.

Let us pray:

For those who mock and torment others and for those who are mocked and tormented;
For all victims of violence and those who commit violence against others;
For those who live under military rule or occupation;

Lord have mercy.
Christ have mercy.
Lord have mercy.

Let us pray:

For ourselves;
When we mock, insult, or hurt others;
When we ourselves are hurt or put down;
That any suffering we may have to endure may be fruitful for ourselves and for others as was Christ's suffering;
And that we may be preserved from indifference to the sufferings of others;

Lord have mercy.
Christ have mercy.
Lord have mercy.

STATION III
Jesus Falls for the First Time

Surely he has borne our infirmities
and carried our diseases;
yet we accounted him stricken,
struck down by God, and afflicted.
—Isaiah 53:4

In Jerusalem, next to the Armenian Catholic Patriarchate, the event commemorated in the Third Station is illustrated on the front of the small chapel that Polish soldiers and refugees built during the Second World War.

Jesus has walked from the Antonia Fortress down the old Transverse Valley to the Tyropoeon Valley road, where he falls for the first time, pinned down by the weight of the crossbeam he is carrying.

To see a strong, young man in such a state is embarrassing, to say the least. Almost instinctively we pass by on the other side, for this is a sight from which men hide their faces. Yet his meek acceptance of this humiliation and weakness is the mighty weapon with which he is disarming sin and suffering and death. Surely we are healed by the punishment he suffered, made whole by the blows he received.

Where Jesus fell, the pushcarts of the merchants may now block our way. We confront the busyness of the marketplace. We confront the commerce and business of our own world. Some people are going to get angry with us for blocking their way, for standing in front of a shop. We

STATION III. JESUS FALLS FOR THE FIRST TIME

may be pushed or shoved. We experience cars driving on this narrow way, taking up almost its entire width. If something unpleasant happens, incorporate it in prayer instead of becoming angry. For certainly Christ would have done so.

We, too, experience physical exhaustion and weakness, and we pray for all who experience moral weakness and failure. Sometimes the burden becomes too much and we falter and fall.

Jesus will fall three times during his walk to Calvary. God falls. God is not supposed to fall, but God does fall. Like the crown of thorns, this is a divine reversal. Everything we hold to be so important—power, physical strength—is turned upside down. God becomes weak, no longer the all-powerful, but one who can fall, one who can die. God becomes human in the person of Jesus, and on the Via Dolorosa we confront the humanity of God in the act of Jesus falling.

We, too, can fall. We, too, can be weak. We, too, can be fully human. We are called on to help and lift up those who have fallen, to embrace the unlovable. For this is what Jesus does for us today as he is forced to carry his cross through the marketplace of Jerusalem.

Let us pray:

For those who are weak and in pain, especially those living with AIDS and other incurable diseases;
For those who experience physical exhaustion;
For those who are weak and sick with hunger;
For those suffering the weakness of advanced age;
For those facing failure;

Lord have mercy.
Christ have mercy.
Lord have mercy.

Let us pray:

For those who care for the physically weak, the sick, the elderly;
For doctors and nurses, social workers, counselors, hospital workers, and families;

Lord have mercy.
Christ have mercy.
Lord have mercy.

Let us pray:

For ourselves;
When we face sickness, physical weakness, tiredness, and exhaustion;
When we experience failure;
That we may know the power of Christ's experience on the Cross;

Lord have mercy.
Christ have mercy.
Lord have mercy.

STATION IV
Jesus Meets His Mother

"This child is destined for the falling and the rising of many in Israel, and to be a sign that will be opposed so that the inner thoughts of many will be revealed—and a sword will pierce your own soul too."

—Luke 2:34b–35

JESUS HAS FALLEN, and now he finds his mother coming forward to help.

This is the one station at which we all have something in common, because we all have been mothered. At the other stations we may have similar concerns, but at this station our relationships with our own mothers provide a bond with Jesus as we reflect on his meeting his mother.

We think about Jesus' mother, Mary, as she saw her Son in agony and in pain, and we lift up all mothers who have to see their sons and their daughters suffer. We know the tremendous pain of parents' seeing their child in pain, seeing their child in any kind of agony. We know the pain of parents who see their child die.

We also have an opportunity at this station to lift up, in our own prayers, difficult times we may have had with our own mothers, times when the relationship was not as we would have liked it to be, times when we have hurt our mothers or times when our mothers have hurt us. At the same time we lift up, in thanksgiving, times of joy and happiness that we have had with our mothers.

As Jesus meets his mother, their love and joy in each other are whole

Station IV. Jesus Meets His Mother

and unblemished. They are one in their love and in their total obedience to the heavenly Father's will. The pain and sorrow of the sacrifice God asks of them now is almost overwhelming.

Here at this station we give thanks for all who have mothered us—family and friends, those who have cared for us. For we are all mothers: both men and women. We are all mothers as we nurture and care for our own children or those who come to us for our motherly love and care. We give thanks for all who have cared for us as we say, "I'm sorry when I have hurt you. Help me to be more Christlike in my relationships. Help me to wear a crown of thorns instead of demanding a crown of gold in my relationships."

Jesus is met by his mother at this station, and her heart is one with his in knowing that his death is to be a sacrifice to bring forgiveness. She knows that in his death he will be bearing the punishment of many and for his sake the Lord will forgive them.

Let us pray:

In thanksgiving for the example, love, and prayers of Our Lady Mary, the Mother of Our Lord;
For our own mothers and fathers, naming them now in our hearts before God, either verbally or in silence;
In thanksgiving for all the love and joy that they have brought to us, and in sorrow for all the ways in which we may have hurt them;
For all who have been "mothers" and "fathers" to us and who still are;
For those living on this side of the narrow curtain of death, and those who have died and are living beyond it;

Lord have mercy.
Christ have mercy.
Lord have mercy.

Let us pray:

For those to whom we are mother or father physically, spiritually, by adoption, or personally, that they may grow in wisdom and stature and in favor with God, with themselves, and with others;

Lord have mercy.
Christ have mercy.
Lord have mercy.

Let us pray:

For ourselves;
As children and as parents, that we may know the love, commitment,
and gentleness of Mary and of Jesus, our Lord, in all our relationships;
And that we, like Mary, may treasure all these things in our hearts;

Lord have mercy.
Christ have mercy.
Lord have mercy.

STATION V
Simon of Cyrene Helps Jesus Carry the Cross

As they led him away, they seized a man, Simon of Cyrene, who was coming from the country, and they laid the cross on him and made him carry it behind Jesus.

—Luke 23:26

JESUS IS STILL UNABLE TO GET TO HIS FEET, so the officer in charge of the execution detail orders an African visitor to Jerusalem, Simon of Cyrene, to carry the crossbeam for him. Relieved of this burden, Jesus is just able to stand and to begin his climb to the city's Gennath Gate.

Have you ever stopped to realize that the Scriptures are color-blind? There is no reference in Scripture to a person's skin color. We do not know the color of Simon of Cyrene's skin. We do not know if he was black; we do not know if he was white; we do not know if he was olive-skinned. All we know is that he came from the area of North Africa that is now called Libya.

At this Fifth Station of the Cross, we are given the opportunity to lift up our own prejudices and fears to God: prejudices and fears that stem from our own weakness, that make us less than human because of the anxieties they provoke.

We become anxious when we encounter someone with a different skin color, a different religious tradition, or a different ethnicity. We lift up and surrender our prejudices and our fears at this station so that we may be healed and live as Christ lived.

STATION V. SIMON OF CYRENE HELPS JESUS CARRY THE CROSS

We accept the invitation to turn upside down the value systems on which much of society is based. This station is another example of the divine reversal. The Scripture is color-blind; all we know is that an African helped Jesus. May we remember that we are all created in the image of God and surrender our own fears when someone is different from us.

Let us pray:

In gratitude that it was an African who helped Jesus on the way to Calvary;
For all the peoples of Africa;
For the newly emerging and developing nations, in Africa and in other parts of the world;
For those nations and peoples still seeking freedom and independence;
For international understanding and cooperation, to foster mutual respect and security between nations;

Lord have mercy.
Christ have mercy.
Lord have mercy.

Let us pray:

For all who suffer because of color, race, or creed;
For the removal of all barriers of resentment and prejudice between peoples;

Lord have mercy.
Christ have mercy.
Lord have mercy.

Let us pray:

For ourselves;
In deepest thanksgiving that God finds us lovable;
That God gave Jesus Christ so that we may have eternal life;
That we may be free from all prejudice based on sex, race, color, religion, or social or economic status;
And be freed from self-love and selfishness in giving, serving, affirming, and nurturing others;

Lord have mercy.
Christ have mercy.
Lord have mercy.

STATION VI
Veronica Wipes Jesus' Brow

He had no form or majesty that
we should look at him,
nothing in his appearance that
we should desire him.
He was despised and rejected
by others;
a man of suffering and
acquainted with infirmity;
and as one from whom others
hide their faces
he was despised, and we held
him of no account.

—Isaiah 53:2–3

Now climbing the steps of the Via Dolorosa, Jesus is almost unable to keep going. The strain, the exhaustion, and the pain show on his face behind its mask of the sweat, blood, and dust that almost blind him.

From her home on this street, a woman sees Jesus approaching. In her compassion for his pain and suffering, she quickly dampens a towel and darts out of her house. Going between the guards, she wipes and cools his ravaged face. Later she will discover an icon of that face marvelously imprinted on her towel; she will come to be known as Veronica. The word *Veronica* means "true icon," and *icon*

STATION VI. VERONICA WIPES JESUS' BROW

means "image." God has sent his Son, the exact likeness (icon) of his own being.

We, too, are created in the image of God. We are created in the icon of God. We also make icons to help us to pray and serve him more effectively. Even more important, we are called ourselves to be icons of God so that when others see us they will see right through us to God and to God's love.

The icon calls us out of ourselves into a more Godlike nature. We are challenged to move beyond who we have been, to live in the fullness of the image of God, to live in that radical discipleship of our Lord, in that more perfect image of God.

At the Sixth Station of the Cross in Jerusalem there is a convent run by the Little Sisters of Jesus. The Sisters always welcome us into the atrium of their tiny chapel, where they sell icons that they have painted to support their ministry to the poorest of the poor.

The Little Sisters of Jesus live out a true image, a Veronica, of God. Society is not very nice to the poorest of the poor. The poorest are rejected. They are despised. They are ignored. But at the Sixth Station of the Cross we are reminded that we are created in the perfect image of God, in the perfect icon of God, and that we can help the poorest of the poor.

How well do we live in that image? We have often been poor representations of our Maker. But now that the Son of God has been sent among us, we not only create icons, but we are called to be icons of God so that when others see us they will see through us to find that very God and to experience God's love.

In her compassion Veronica sees through the horror and ugliness to the beauty of Jesus. She seems to know instinctively that it is the Lord who has made the punishment fall on him, the punishment all of us deserved.

The Sixth Station of the Cross comes not from Scripture, but from the hearts of European people in the Middle Ages, who constructed Stations of the Cross in their own cities in Europe because they could not go to Jerusalem. Veronica is a spokeswoman for them and for us. As the Scripture takes Jesus from his judgment to his crucifixion, she comes forward from our hearts to wipe the blood, sweat, and dust from his face.

Let us pray:

In thanksgiving for all who see with God's eyes, and who recognize love
and beauty where we may see only ugliness and squalor;
For every act and occasion of compassion and caring;
And for all who feel for God in those who are suffering;

Lord have mercy.
Christ have mercy.
Lord have mercy.

Let us pray:

For all whose suffering, pain, deprivation, and degradation make them
ugly and unattractive to themselves and to others;
For all who have the courage to love and show compassion;

Lord have mercy.
Christ have mercy.
Lord have mercy.

Let us pray:

For ourselves;
That our eyes may be opened to see beauty where God sees beauty;
That we may be given a heart open to compassion and hands ready to
comfort and console;
That others may see in us a true icon of God;

Lord have mercy.
Christ have mercy.
Lord have mercy.

STATION VII
Jesus Falls a Second Time

He himself bore our sins in his body on the cross, so that, free from sins, we might live for righteousness; by his wounds you have been healed.

—1 Peter 2:24

THE SIGHT OF HIS MOTHER, the aid of Simon of Cyrene, and Veronica's comfort have helped Jesus walk a little farther. But nothing can sustain the strength of the doomed prisoner for long. At the top of the Via Dolorosa he falls for the second time.

In Jesus' day a city gate stood at the spot where the Via Dolorosa feeds into the original main road of Jerusalem, the Cardo. It was not unknown for the Roman authorities to let the condemned get to this gate before granting them a pardon or commutation of their sentence, so the execution detail holds the procession here for a while. But Pilate has granted the one and only pardon this day to Barabbas. Jesus knows this. There is no pardon for the supreme pardoner: No one in authority cares about his fate. Willingly he gives himself to be wounded because of our sins.

Jesus knows that the way he is walking is irrevocable now. It is the way to his death. Even though Simon of Cyrene is carrying his cross, Jesus' energy is running out. His time is running out.

Jesus' falls at the Third, Seventh, and Ninth Stations of the Cross are human and humbling moments for him on the Via Dolorosa to death. Like the moments with Veronica, accounts of the falls do not come

Station VII. Jesus Falls a Second Time

from the Gospels. They come from medieval Europeans who created Stations of the Cross out of their own imagination when they could not go to Jerusalem. Wars and plagues had taught them what suffering and death are. They understood what falling is. In their minds they saw Jesus fall, too. They felt his falls were holy, and they believed his falls made them holy along with him. They knew his resurrection was coming and that they would rise with him as they had fallen with him.

As we walk along the Via Dolorosa today, some passersby may feel something holy in our presence. Some may come up and touch us, or touch the cross we are carrying, and cross themselves. This practice goes back to the early Byzantine days, when people came to this land not only to visit holy places but to be with holy people and to venerate them. Today as we carry the cross through the streets of Jerusalem, some will see us as holy people; some will want to be in our presence for their own sanctification. When this happens we accept it in our prayers.

Let us pray:
In humility and gratitude for God's mercy and forgiveness;
That mercy may always temper justice;
For heads of state, parole boards, and those who have responsibility for showing official mercy;
For all who seek pardon and mercy;
Lord have mercy.
Christ have mercy.
Lord have mercy.

Let us pray:
For those who suffer mental weakness and fatigue;
For the mentally ill, the anxious, the lonely, and the distressed;
For those suffering from senility;
And for all who care for them, their families, friends, and members of the caring professions;
Lord have mercy.
Christ have mercy.
Lord have mercy.

Let us pray:

For ourselves;
That we may be forgiving and merciful;
For those we have hurt or offended;
And that whenever we see someone in pain we may recognize Christ in them and Christ in us;

Lord have mercy.
Christ have mercy.
Lord have mercy.

STATION VIII
Jesus Talks to the Weeping Women

A great number of the people followed him, and among them were women who were beating their breasts and wailing for him. But Jesus turned to them and said, "Daughters of Jerusalem, do not weep for me, but weep for yourselves and for your children. For the days are surely coming when they will say, 'Blessed are the barren, and the wombs that never bore, and the breasts that never nursed.' Then they will begin to say to the mountains, 'Fall on us'; and to the hills, 'Cover us.' For if they do this when the wood is green, what will happen when it is dry?"

—Luke 23:27–31

SEEING THAT NO LAST-MINUTE PARDON IS COMING for any of their prisoners, the execution escort prepares to get the condemned men moving again. Realizing what this means, some women who have accompanied the procession begin to mourn and wail aloud. Their compassion is always aroused by the sight of beaten and abused men being driven or dragged to execution. But their compassion for Jesus is heightened by their recognition that he is the innocent victim of the political machinations of their own leaders and of the representatives of the Roman occupying power.

Jesus turns to them. "Daughters of Jerusalem," he says, "do not weep for me." Jesus' death is not the accidental by-product of contemporary politics. It is a deliberate act of self-giving. He tells the women of Jerusalem not to weep for him but for themselves.

STATION VIII. JESUS TALKS TO THE WEEPING WOMEN

In modern times, the Eighth Station is marked only by a slice of pillar embedded in the street wall and inscribed with the Greek letters *NIKA,* for "Jesus Christ Conquers."

Jerusalem has always known pain, and it has always known the tears of women—Armenian women, Jewish women, Palestinian women, Druze women—as they have waited and have watched their husbands, their sons and daughters, their brothers and sisters, go off to the slaughter of war or to the punishment of prisons and detention centers.

Today in the Church of the Holy Sepulchre, built over Golgotha, or Calvary, there is a chapel called Christ's Prison. To this day, women (and men) come to light candles for their sons, spouses, brothers, and lovers who are being held in prison. They weep as they pray that a pardon may come to their loved ones.

The women of Jerusalem knew that no pardon had come for Jesus at the city gate, the place where a pardon sometimes was delivered. So they wept for him, but he told them to weep for themselves instead.

And Jesus tells us not to weep for him, but to weep for ourselves in our injustices and in our cruelty.

Let us pray:

For all women everywhere;

Especially for those who have to watch husbands, sons, daughters, sisters, brothers, friends, or lovers go to war;

For those who mourn loved ones killed or wounded in violence not of their own making;

For the women of Jerusalem today: Jews, Christians, Muslims, Palestinians, Arabs, Israelis, Armenians, and others;

And for the women we know in our own lives and who are standing beside us;

Lord have mercy.
Christ have mercy.
Lord have mercy.

Let us pray:

In penitence and sorrow for each time right is obscured by might;
For every time the powerful are given undue respect while the weak and
powerless, the poor and dispossessed, are ignored and repressed;
We pray for liberation for women and for liberation of men;

Lord have mercy.
Christ have mercy.
Lord have mercy.

Let us pray:

For ourselves;
That the Holy Spirit will give us the mind of Christ
to love and respect those who are oppressed;
And to know Christ's dignity when we are made to suffer indignity;

Lord have mercy.
Christ have mercy.
Lord have mercy.

STATION IX
Jesus Falls a Third Time

For we do not have a high priest who is unable to sympathize with our weaknesses, but we have one who in every respect has been tested as we are, yet is without sin. Let us therefore approach the throne of grace with boldness, so that we may receive mercy and find grace to help in time of need.

—Hebrews 4:15–16

THE EXECUTION PROCESSION HAS COME OUT OF THE CITY GATE into an area called Golgotha, or Calvary. This is the unused quarry that Herod the Great made into a public place so people could see the executions and learn the dreadful lesson that the crucifixions are intended to teach.

But often passersby are indifferent. On that busy Passover eve, how many people do you think really cared that another three men were going to be crucified? Very few, I suspect. The Roman guard, the sentenced men carrying their crosses, and the crowd following the procession add congestion to the busy street when everyone is hurrying home. There is a lot to do before tomorrow.

And we, standing in the Cardo where the main entrance to the Church of the Holy Sepulchre once stood, are going to experience some indifference ourselves. Some will try to weave their way around us, not experiencing any feelings toward us whatsoever. To them we are just another tour group on the streets of Jerusalem, and they are very busy.

How often do we try to avoid those around us on a city street or even in church on Sunday? We are very busy. We have a lot to do in our

STATION IX. JESUS FALLS A THIRD TIME

important lives, and we cannot take the time to stop and get involved in someone else's life, someone who may need us just to listen to them for a moment.

At this station, Jesus falls for the third time; we fall whenever we pass by a person who needs us. Jesus has become the lamb about to be slaughtered, the sheep about to be sheared, and he never says a word. Though he, of the three sentenced to die, seems least able to withstand the pain and awful humiliation, he endures it humbly; he never says a word. How often have we passed indifferently by such a person?

Let us pray:

For those who experience moral weakness and failure;
For those who know what it is to lose their faith;
For those who have lost hope in this world or the next;
For those who are at the very limits of their mental, physical, spiritual, or moral strength;

Lord have mercy.
Christ have mercy.
Lord have mercy.

Let us pray:

For those who counsel the despairing or suicidal;
For chaplains and those who minister in prisons;

Lord have mercy.
Christ have mercy.
Lord have mercy.

Let us pray:

For ourselves;
When we know moral failure;
When everything and everyone seems to be against us and hope flees;
That we may remember Jesus waiting for crucifixion and know his patience, presence, and resolve;

Lord have mercy.
Christ have mercy.
Lord have mercy.

STATION X
Jesus Is Stripped of His Garments

When the soldiers had crucified Jesus, they took his clothes and divided them into four parts, one for each soldier. They also took his tunic; now the tunic was seamless, woven in one piece from the top. So they said to one another, "Let us not tear it, but cast lots for it to see who will get it." This was to fulfill what the scripture says, "They divided my clothes among themselves, and for my clothing they cast lots."

—John 19:23–24

WE HAVE ARRIVED AT THE CHURCH built over the quarry rocks where Jesus' cross was once planted, and we stand in its Calvary Balcony, where a mosaic of Abraham offering his son Isaac foreshadows the sacrifice of Christ by God.

Here Jesus was stripped of his clothes. For him, this is perhaps the most terrible moment in the whole appalling day. As a Jew he has been taught never to be seen naked. To be exposed to the curiosity of anyone and everyone passing by is one of the worst things that can happen. His humiliation, his degradation, is virtually complete. Only the absolute helplessness of being stretched on the cross remains.

We, the crowd, despise and reject him; to us he now appears as nothing, so totally without dignity as a human being does he appear. Yet it is *our* degradation that he is bearing. He is stripped naked before us so that when we stand totally exposed for who and what we are before the Ultimate Judge, we shall not need to be ashamed. He is

STATION X. JESUS IS STRIPPED OF HIS GARMENTS

undergoing suffering that rightly should have been ours.

We stop to think of the many times we have stripped other people of their dignity, of their human worth, just so we might feel a little bit better ourselves. We think how often men strip women, how often men rape women for their own gratification, how men take away women's dignity, so that they might feel more manly.

We remember Jesus' being stripped of his garments, and we offer up the times when we, too, have stripped other people. We ask God's forgiveness.

Let us pray:
At the Tenth Station we pray for those who are exposed to ridicule, who are shamed, humiliated, degraded;
For battered wives and battered children;
For women who are raped and for children who are victims of violence and sexual abuse;

Lord have mercy.
Christ have mercy.
Lord have mercy.

Let us pray:
For those who expose, shame, humiliate, and degrade others, by word or action or simply in their thoughts;
For those who degrade or exploit others racially, sexually, intellectually, or economically;

Lord have mercy.
Christ have mercy.
Lord have mercy.

Let us pray:
For ourselves;
When we are ashamed or abused;
That we may find healing and so live that we have nothing to hide;

Lord have mercy.
Christ have mercy.
Lord have mercy.

STATION XI
Jesus Is Crucified

Those who passed by derided him, shaking their heads and saying, "You who would destroy the temple and build it in three days, save yourself! If you are the Son of God, come down from the cross."

—Matthew 27:39–40

AFTER THE HUMILIATION OF NAKEDNESS, Jesus is subjected to the physical agony of having great spikes hammered through his wrists to stake his arms upon the crossbeam on which he lies. The beam is then raised until it fits into its socket in the upright beam. Jesus hangs suspended from the spikes hammered through his wrists. A third great spike is driven through his ankles.

Since every crucified person is labeled with a placard, Jesus' cross bears a placard reading, "Jesus of Nazareth, King of the Jews." The Judean authorities do not like the wording but Pilate, disgusted, insists that it remain as he had dictated. Members of the crowd jeer or are silently appalled.

Jesus himself says, "Father, forgive them, for they do not know what they are doing" (Luke 23:34). Those who hear him do not know that it is because of our sins that he is pierced and that we die with him on his cross. They do not know that nails are not what hold him to the cross but rather his life-giving love for us.

Three condemned men hang on their crosses, slowly dying. But it is the man in the middle who holds everyone's attention, even that of his

STATION XI. JESUS IS CRUCIFIED

companions in agony. One of these two joins the mockers in the crowd and screams insults at him. The other man protests and, perhaps even to his own astonishment, acknowledges that Jesus really is a king. Despite his own weakness and pain, Jesus turns his head toward this man, saying, "I promise you that today you will be in paradise with me."

Let us pray:

In awe and gratitude we stand before the mystery of the Cross;
Here we know that God loved the world so much that God gave his Son to this kind of suffering and this kind of death;
That Jesus accepted this suffering and death out of love for us so that we may share his risen life;
We acclaim Jesus as the Christ, fountain of our salvation and healing;

Lord have mercy.
Christ have mercy.
Lord have mercy.

Let us pray:

For those who would destroy that which is good, that which is sacred, beautiful, and true;
For every attempt to suppress the truth and good news of Christ crucified and for all who are persecutors of Christ's Church and God's children in the world;
For those who are persecuted or oppressed for any reason;

Lord have mercy.
Christ have mercy.
Lord have mercy.

Let us pray:

For ourselves;
Whenever we are called to account for our faith;
That we may understand and incorporate into our lives the Way of the Cross, allowing sin, suffering, and death to be broken on the rock of love, and refusing to retaliate against evil with evil;

Lord have mercy.
Christ have mercy.
Lord have mercy.

STATION XII
Jesus Dies on the Cross

Then Jesus gave a loud cry and breathed his last. And the curtain of the temple was torn in two, from top to bottom. Now when the centurion, who stood facing him, saw that in this way he breathed his last, he said, "Truly this man was God's Son!"

—Mark 15:37–39

THE CHURCH OF THE HOLY SEPULCHRE WAS BUILT over an ancient stone quarry that, in Jesus' day, lay just outside the city walls. Ever since the eighth century B.C., limestone had been quarried from this pit. But there is a flawed strain of limestone in this quarry. The church balcony where we stand for the Twelfth Station contains a circular opening in the floor through which we reach down and touch the actual spoiled rock, the stone not worth quarrying. We recall the Psalmist's words: "The stone which the builder rejected has become the head of the corner" (Psalm 118:22). The divine reversal is under way. This crucified man whom the crowds jeered will indeed become the "head of the corner." The cornerstone of the church is placed on this rejected stone.

At Jesus' cross a little band of grieving figures stands. To one of them, his mother, Jesus says gently, indicating the disciple whom he loves, "He is your son." And to that youngest disciple he says, "She is your mother."

Only then does he give some small sign of his own distress. "I am thirsty," he says. Then that distress deepens, and Jesus groans the prayer of Psalm 22, "My God, My God, why do you abandon me?" Death is not

STATION XII. JESUS DIES ON THE CROSS

far from him now. The other two men are enduring their execution strongly, but Jesus is visibly weakening. "Father," he whispers, "in your hands I place my spirit."

Suddenly his face changes and he cries out in a great voice, "It is finished. It is accomplished! All that the Father sent me to do I have accomplished!" He dies. And his executioner has the last word: "This man was really the son of God!"

Let us pray:

For the dying;
For ourselves, in our last days, in our last hour;
In gratitude that because of the loneliness of Jesus on the cross no one need ever die alone or without hope;

Lord have mercy.
Christ have mercy.
Lord have mercy.

Let us pray:

For those who care for the dying: their families, friends, nurses, doctors, counselors, and the communion of saints;
For all hospices for the dying;

Lord have mercy.
Christ have mercy.
Lord have mercy.

Let us pray:

For all persons who have died, whoever they may be;
That they may know Jesus and share his risen and eternal life;

Lord have mercy.
Christ have mercy.
Lord have mercy.

STATION XIII
Jesus' Body Is Taken Down from the Cross

After these things, Joseph of Arimathea, who was a disciple of Jesus, though a secret one because of his fear of the Jews, asked Pilate to let him take away the body of Jesus. Pilate gave him permission; so he came and removed his body. Nicodemus, who had at first come to Jesus by night, also came, bringing a mixture of myrrh and aloes, weighing about a hundred pounds. They took the body of Jesus and wrapped it with the spices in linen clothes, according to the custom of the Jews. Now there was a garden in the place where he was crucified, and in the garden there was a new tomb in which no one had ever been laid. And so, because it was the Jewish day of Preparation and the tomb was nearby, they laid Jesus there.

—John 19:38–42

THE EXPERIENCED COMMANDER OF THE EXECUTION SQUAD knows that he must give his prisoners the coup de grâce and have their bodies removed before sundown; he orders his men to break the legs of the crucified men. To the commander's surprise, Jesus seems already dead, but he insists on confirming the fact by thrusting his spear into Jesus' side.

As the bodies are about to be taken down and thrown into a mass grave, two local dignitaries arrive with an order from the governor allowing them to remove Jesus' body and to bury it privately. The two, Joseph and Nicodemus, remove the iron spikes and lower Jesus' bloody, grimy, sweat-caked body into the arms of his mother and the tiny band of watchers.

STATION XIII. JESUS' BODY IS TAKEN DOWN FROM THE CROSS

Do any of them remember what he had said only the night before, "This, my body, given for you... This, my blood, poured out for you"? Countless millions will hear those words someday and remember. But the future is hidden from the mourners at this moment.

By now it is too late in the day to complete the preparation of Jesus' body for burial before the Sabbath begins. Therefore the body is taken to the nearby tomb owned by Joseph of Arimathea, who had helped achieve the release of the body. Now it awaits preparation for proper burial after the Sabbath.

In the Church of the Holy Sepulchre, two different spots honor this Station of the Cross. One is on the church balcony built over the rejected rock of Calvary. The other site is called the Crusader Stone of Anointing, facing the front doors of the church. To this day, people like to bring the shrouds they have purchased for their own burials, lay them on this spot, and pour anointing oils upon them.

For Jesus, all of the suffering, all of the pain, is over. All the words that could be spoken have been spoken. Now we are left with silence. Now we are left with our innermost thoughts. Now we are left with the words of the centurion, "Truly this man was the Son of God."

Let us pray:

For the dead;
Especially those we have known and loved, remembering them
in our hearts;
For those who have influenced us for good;

Lord have mercy.
Christ have mercy.
Lord have mercy.

Let us pray:

For those who mourn;
For those who care for the bereaved;
For the healing of pain and grief;

Lord have mercy.
Christ have mercy.
Lord have mercy.

Let us pray:

For ourselves;
Whenever we eat the bread and drink the cup of salvation;
In thanksgiving that Jesus Christ gave his body to be broken for us and his blood to be shed for us;
That we may be enabled and strengthened by his Spirit to give ourselves to be broken and poured out for others, for the sanctification of the whole of God's creation;

Lord have mercy.
Christ have mercy.
Lord have mercy.

STATION XIV
Jesus' Body Is Placed in the Tomb

So Joseph took the body and wrapped it in a clean linen cloth and laid it in his own new tomb, which he had hewn in the rock. He then rolled a great stone to the door of the tomb and went away. Mary Magdalene and the other Mary were there sitting opposite the tomb.

—Matthew 27:59–61

WE GO, FINALLY, TO THE SMALL BUILDING CALLED THE EMPTY TOMB, inside the great Church of the Holy Sepulchre, to lift up our prayers.

What other church, what other cathedral, what other basilica in the world hosts an Empty Tomb?

None other does. Such a church is found only in Jerusalem. Our roots stem from this Empty Tomb.

This Empty Tomb makes sense out of our lives.

This Empty Tomb gives meaning and purpose to our lives.

This Empty Tomb makes us all citizens of Jerusalem—not only this earthly Jerusalem, but also the heavenly Jerusalem, where we look forward to feasting on the heavenly bread.

So as we stand before the Empty Tomb, let us make our confession.

Station XIV. Jesus' Body Is Placed in the Tomb

L: Lord, Jesus Christ,
   we come to confess our feelings.

R: We come with anxiety and sorrow,
   with hope and expectation.

L: Lord, Jesus Christ,
   we come to the lonely cross

R: And we see you stripped,
   we see you murdered,
   we see you deserted.

L: Lord, Jesus Christ,
   we come to the Empty Tomb

R: And we see our own death,
   we see our own tomb,
   we see our own emptiness.

L: Lord, Jesus Christ,
   when we come to the Empty Tomb

R: We remember how we treated
   our parents,
   our friends,
   our neighbors,
   our Lord,
   and we feel sorry
   for ourselves.

L: Lord, Jesus Christ,
   when we come to the Empty Tomb

R: We see a hungry world before us,
   the pain of starving children,
   the guilt of war on our hands,

the terror of friends without rights,
and we know that we share in these evils.

L: Lord, Jesus Christ,
when we come to the Empty Tomb

R: We search inside ourselves
and we cannot escape what we are,
people caught in our selfish love,
our cold hypocrisy,
our depressions,
our loneliness,
and our frustrations.

L: Lord, Jesus Christ,
when we come to the Empty Tomb

R: We face you as never before,
as the one forgotten,
as the one oppressed,
as the one pushed aside,
as the one left out.

L: Lord, Jesus Christ,
we come to the Empty Tomb

R: To confess our guilt,
our pain,
our emptiness,
and to look for hope
from you.

But it is also at the Empty Tomb that we receive our healing:

L: People of God,
why do you seek the living
among the dead?

R: Because we are afraid,
we are uncertain,
we are uncomfortable here,
and we have doubts about this man.

L: Do not be afraid,
for he has risen from the dead,
he has broken through the tomb,
he has come back to life,
and he is here among us now.

People of God,
why do you seek the living
among the dead?

R: Because we feel guilty,
we feel lonely,
and we feel lost,
for we deserted that man.

L: Do not carry your guilt any longer,
for he has taken the guilt himself,
he has buried it in his grave,
he has lifted it to his cross,
and he is here among us now.

People of God,
why do you seek the living
among the dead?

R: Because our wounds are deep,
we have torn away from that man,
we have broken with him
and with our brothers and sisters.

L: Do not dwell on your wounds
for he has risen to heal you,

he has risen to forgive you,
he has risen to change you all,
and bind us all together now.

People of God,
he is not here; he is risen.

R: Yes, he is risen!

L: He is risen!

R: And he is here!

L: Alleluia!

R: Alleluia!

L: He is risen!

R: And he is here!